# Umlaut, Prince of Düsseldorf

The Coarse Acting *Hamlet*

Michael Green

A Samuel French Acting Edition

SAMUELFRENCH.COM
SAMUELFRENCH-LONDON.CO.UK

Copyright © 2012 by Michael Green
All Rights Reserved

*UMLAUT, PRINCE OF DÜSSELDORF* is fully protected under the copyright laws of the United States of America, the British Commonwealth, including Canada, and all other countries of the Copyright Union. All rights, including professional and amateur stage productions, recitation, lecturing, public reading, motion picture, radio broadcasting, television and the rights of translation into foreign languages are strictly reserved.

ISBN 978-0-573-12291-0

www.SamuelFrench.com
www.SamuelFrench-London.co.uk

---

### For Production Enquiries

**United States and Canada**
Info@SamuelFrench.com
1-866-598-8449

**United Kingdom and Europe**
Theatre@SamuelFrench-London.co.uk
020-7255-4302

Each title is subject to availability from Samuel French, depending upon country of performance. Please be aware that *UMLAUT, PRINCE OF DÜSSELDORF* may not be licensed by Samuel French in your territory. Professional and amateur producers should contact the nearest Samuel French office or licensing partner to verify availability.

---

CAUTION: Professional and amateur producers are hereby warned that *UMLAUT, PRINCE OF DÜSSELDORF* is subject to a licensing fee. Publication of this play(s) does not imply availability for performance. Both amateurs and professionals considering a production are strongly advised to apply to Samuel French before starting rehearsals, advertising, or booking a theatre. A licensing fee must be paid whether the title(s) is presented for charity or gain and whether or not admission is charged. Professional/Stock licensing rights are controlled by Sheil Land Associates, 52 Doughty Street, London WC1N 2LS.

No one shall make any changes in this title(s) for the purpose of production. No part of this book may be reproduced, stored in a retrieval system, or transmitted in any form, by any means, now known or yet to be invented, including mechanical, electronic, photocopying, recording, videotaping, or otherwise, without the prior written permission of the publisher. No one shall upload this title(s), or part of this title(s), to any social media websites.

For all enquiries regarding motion picture, television, and other media rights, please contact Samuel French.

## MUSIC USE NOTE

Licensees are solely responsible for obtaining formal written permission from copyright owners to use copyrighted music in the performance of this play and are strongly cautioned to do so. If no such permission is obtained by the licensee, then the licensee must use only original music that the licensee owns and controls. Licensees are solely responsible and liable for all music clearances and shall indemnify the copyright owners of the play(s) and their licensing agent, Samuel French, against any costs, expenses, losses and liabilities arising from the use of music by licensees. Please contact the appropriate music licensing authority in your territory for the rights to any incidental music.

## IMPORTANT BILLING AND CREDIT REQUIREMENTS

If you have obtained performance rights to this title, please refer to your licensing agreement for important billing and credit requirements.

## CHARACTERS

**Klaus**, King of Düsseldorf
**Wilhelmina**, his wife and Queen
**Umlaut**, her son by her previous marriage to the late king
**Ghost**, of the former king
**Gezundheit**, Chancellor
**Hildegard**, his daughter
**Heineken**, Umlaut's friend and an officer
**Budweiser**
**Kronenbourg** } soldiers
**Rosenstern**
**Guildencranz** } spies
**Anthrax**, a courtier
**Clown**, a gravedigger
**First Player**
**Courtiers, Attendants, Strolling Players** etc.

Time — at director's discretion

# INTRODUCTION

Taking liberties with Shakespeare has a long and distinguished history. In the 18th Century some plays were rewritten to have a happy ending and the custom of revising them has continued to the present day. The most dreaded words in the theatre are when the director announces, "I see this play as ..." He or she then describes how they have changed the period, altered the text, mutilated a famous speech, moved the locale, invented two new scenes and added a pop group.

I feel therefore I need not apologize for any liberties taken in this little spoof. As long ago as the sixties I remember Macbeth being shot by a firing squad at the Theatre Royal, East London. More recently elsewhere I recall the ghost in *Hamlet* appearing in a modern business suit to his son, who was smoking a cigarette. Then there was the production where Fortinbras arrived on a motorcycle, complete with crash helmet. This raised a huge laugh, in striking contrast to the gravediggers, who had spoken their jokes in complete silence. I have also seen a version of *Titus Andronicus* in modern dress where the famous banquet scene in which Tamora eats a pie made from the flesh of her two murdered sons, was played as a cocktail party, with Tamora politely nibbling at a canapé, presumably smeared with her children. Some of the cast suggested new dialogue: Guest: I don't like children. Titus: Well, leave them and just eat the chips.

I write as one who has carried a machine pistol in *Two Gentlemen of Verona* and worn a swastika in *Measure for Measure*.

So if anyone requires motivation for a performance of *Umlaut, Prince of Düsseldorf*, I suggest they think of it as put on by a group from Bogthorpe University directed and freely adapted by a lecturer in media studies who claimed the original was based on an old German manuscript. The stage manager vanished just before the dress rehearsal and the play had to be cut savagely because at the Edinburgh Fringe they could only secure a half hour slot in a basement room in Bruntsfield.

Or not. Personally I always find the best motivation is a few hundred quid.

**Michael Green**

## NOTES FOR DIRECTORS

There is no mystery about Coarse Acting. It is basically an impersonation of a performance of a play by an incompetent or disaster-prone company. The title comes from my book *The Art Of Coarse Acting* wherein there are various definitions of a Coarse Actor, such as one who know the lines but not the order in which they come, or who plays every part with a limp (sometimes on both legs simultaneously). Or he may be disaster-prone, like the man I know who was stuck on stage by a jammed door and escaped by going through the fireplace.

One of the laws of Coarse Acting is that the more serious the drama, the funnier it is when pretension is exploded by some unexpected disaster. People find it funny when actors are in trouble. Like farce, Coarse Acting is tragedy played at high speed, so the cast must plough on with deadly seriousness as the show collapses around then.

I haven't specified any particular period for this play in common with current practice of setting Shakespeare in any century. Traditional or timeless would be fine, and don't worry about the anomalies of the ghost in armour or the playing of the German national anthem. Shakespeare is full of them. However, I always feel there is a strong affinity between the court at Elsinore and the dark days of Germany with Hitler or the Kaiser and Bismark. Setting it in Nazi Germany might be a possibility, with the King sporting a toothbrush moustache and the ghost in a gas-mask. Even better might be the late 19th Century, with actors in spiked helmets and waxed moustaches. The main thing is a strong German atmosphere, or rather the atmosphere of Germany as portrayed in Hollywood films, all heel clicking and saluting.

As regards the acting, desperate sincerity is the keynote. Perhaps too desperate in some cases. Pace is important, too. Nothing is less funny than a Coarse Acting play that drags. Half the fun of this spoof is that the world's greatest play is condensed from four hours to twenty-odd minutes. In particular, the salutes when the King drinks, consisting of cannon, drums and *Deutschland Über Alles* must be short — not more than seven or eight seconds. The salute might get even quicker as the play progresses, ending in a screech.

A lot of business is closely detailed in the stage directions. Read these carefully, and don't cut business without good reason. You may need the laughs. Of course, directors can add their own. I recall with great pleasure a production of another Coarse play in which one character stood up every time he spoke and then sat down.

Remember that any accidental hitches aren't funny. Real disasters, as distinct from those planned, kill the joke, and audiences sense it. One of the unfunniest evenings I've ever spent at the theatre came when the set really did fall down in a Coarse Acting play. Hence the need for careful rehearsal.

Perhaps not surprisingly, genuine Coarse actors are rarely funny in the deliberate version. The best actors are the best actors.

Good luck.

**Michael Green**

Other titles by Michael Green
published by Samuel French Ltd:

The Art of Coarse Acting

Four Plays for Coarse Actors
(Comprising *All's Well That Ends As You Like It*,
*A Collier's Tuesday Tea*, *Il Fornicazione* and *Streuth*)

The Coarse Acting Show 2
(Comprising *The Cherry Sisters*, *Henry the Tenth Part
Seven*, *Last Call for Breakfast* and *Moby Dick*)

The Third Great Coarse Acting Show
(Comprising *A Fish In Her Kettle*, *Julius and Cleopatra*,
*Present Slaughter*, *Stalag 69* and *The Vagabond Prince*)

Coarse Acting Strikes Back
(Comprising *Cinderella*, *Oedocles King of Thebes*,
*Pride at Southanger Park* and *Trapped!*)

# UMLAUT, PRINCE OF DÜSSELDORF

## Scene 1

*The battlements of the royal castle in Düsseldorf*

*The stage is in darkness. The Lights slowly come up. Then the howling of wind is heard and the stage is filled with dense smoke. Budweiser is alone on stage, armed with a lance and in a state of readiness*

**Budweiser** (*calling off*) Is Heineken there?

*Heineken and Kronenbourg enter with lances, groping through the fog with difficulty*

**Heineken** A piece of him.
**Budweiser** Welcome, good Heineken. Welcome, stout Kronenbourg.
**Kronenbourg** What, has this thing appeared again, noble Budweiser?
**Budweiser** I have seen nothing.
**Kronenbourg** Heineken says 'tis but imagination.
**Heineken** Tush t'will not appear.
**Budweiser** Donner und blitzen! I tell you I saw it last night. Just as the bell struck one.
**Heineken** Peace. Look where it comes again. (*He points excitedly to one side*)

*All turn to face offstage, lances ready*

*Enter Ghost. He is in armour with helmet and visor open. He drags a long length of chain behind him to show he is a ghost. He is accompanied by an extra puff of smoke and a green spot*

*Unfortunately Ghost comes on behind the group, who don't notice him ("I thought we changed it at the dress rehearsal old chap"). Ghost gives a moan to attract their attention. They turn*

**Budweiser**  In the same figure as the king that's dead.
**Kronenbourg**  It is most like the former king.
**Budweiser**  They say the spirits of the dead converse in Latin. Heineken, thou art a scholar. Speak to it in Latin tongue.
**Heineken**  Hic, haec, hoc.

*Ghost turns away as a cock crows*

**Budweiser**  It is offended.
**Kronenbourg**  See it stalks away.
**Heineken**  Stay. Speak, speak. I charge thee, speak. Stop it, Budweiser!
**Budweiser**  Shall I strike it with my spear?
**Heineken**  Do if it will not stand.
**Budweiser**  'Tis here.
**Kronenbourg**  'Tis here.
**Heineken**  Nay, 'tis there.

*Confusion as they rush around in the fog. Ghost is stabbed in the bottom by mistake*

   *Ghost exits, dragging its chain, moaning and holding its buttocks*

**Heineken**  Umlaut, the old king's son, must know of this. Until then, stout Kronenbourg and honest Budweiser, not a word to anyone.

   *Exeunt coughing*

## Scene 2

*The court*

*There are two thrones on stage*

*A flourish. Enter Klaus, King of Düsseldorf, wearing a huge gown, Queen Wilhelmina, Prince Umlaut, Gezundheit and his son Grolsch and Courtiers including Cup Bearer holding a huge goblet of wine*

**King**  Though yet of our dear brother's death the memory
Be green, yet let us mourn no longer.
Be jocund, merry as he would have wished.
Behold I drink to his memory.

*Cup Bearer brings him wine. He tosses the drink down and throws away the goblet which hits Cup Bearer in the face. Just as well it's made from some harmless substance such as papier mâché (the cup, not the face)*

**Gezundheit**  My lord, I crave a suit.
**King**  Worthy Chancellor Gezundheit, 'tis already granted. We know thy worth.
**Gezundheit**  'Tis for my son, young Grolsch. He wishes leave to go to France.
**Grolsch**  I returned for your coronation, my liege, but now my duty's done.
**King**  Then go with the King's blessing.

*Gezundheit and Grolsch withdraw only to be met by an unexpected jet of smoke as they leave the stage. This forces them to grope for another exit*

*The King's gaze lights on Umlaut who is standing apart brooding*

**King**  Now good Umlaut, do the clouds still hang on you?

*The Queen gets up and goes to Umlaut*

**Queen**  Good Umlaut, dearest son, do not leave us now to go to Wittenberg. Stay here with your mother and her new husband.
**Umlaut**  I shall in all my best obey you, madam.
**King**  Why, 'tis a loving and a fair reply.
In grace whereof
No jocund health that we do drink today
But the great cannon to the clouds shall tell.
Come away.

*Cannon and drums sound, followed by two bars of "Deutschland über Alles", played at high speed. The music ends in a screech. All stand to attention and salute. Once more the King throws his goblet in the face of his long-suffering Cup Bearer. He then rises but gets his feet entangled in his gown and falls, being saved by crashing into the Cup Bearer who receives further injuries in the fall*

*Exeunt all except Umlaut*

**Umlaut**  Within two months my father dead, my mother to my uncle married. (*He pronounces it "marry-ed"*) Would I were buried. (*He pronounces it "bury-ed". He puts his face in his hands*)

*Enter Heineken, Kronenbourg and Budweiser*

**Heineken**  My lord, last night I think I saw your father.
**Umlaut**  The King? My father? Where?
**Heineken**  Upon the battlements. I spoke in Latin but answer made he none. Then the morning cock crew and he vanished.
**Umlaut**  Perchance it was a ghost. Hold you the watch tonight?
**All**  We do, my lord.
**Umlaut**  I will watch tonight with you upon the platform 'twixt eleven and twelve. Farewell.

*Exeunt all but Umlaut*

*The thrones are struck*

**Umlaut**  Something is rotten in the State of Düsseldorf.

*Umlaut exits but at the last moment realizes he should have gone off the other side and hastily corrects*

## Scene 3

*Enter Gezundheit, Grolsch and Hildegard*

**Gezundheit**  (*embracing Grolsch*) There — my blessing. And now aboard for France.
**Grolsch**  Farewell, Father. (*He kisses his sister*) Farewell, sister. (*He kisses his father*) Remember what I told you, sister.
**Hildegard**  Farewell, brother. (*She embraces her father*)

*All three madly exchange kisses and embraces in an effort to end the confusion*

*Exit Grolsch*

**Gezundheit**  What is it, daughter, that he hath told you?
**Hildegard**  Something touching the Lord Umlaut.
**Gezundheit**  Marry, well bethought. The Lord Umlaut has been too familiar with you. Trust not his tenders of affection. Guard well your chaste treasure from him. (*He cackles lasciviously and glances at the chaste treasure before patting her bottom*)
**Hildegard**  I shall obey my lord.

*Hildegard exits*

**Gezundheit**  Yet I do fear thy nature is too full of the milk of human kindness.

*Gezundheit exits*

SCENE 4

*The battlements*

*Enter Umlaut, Heineken and Budweiser. Wind howls*

**Umlaut**  What hour now?
**Heineken**  It lacks of twelve.
**Budweiser**  No, it is struck.

*Sudden sound of trumpets, cannon and two or three bars of "Deutschland über Alles", plus cheering. All stand to attention and salute*

**Heineken**  What means this?
**Umlaut**  The King doth make carouse. At every drink
   The cannon and the trumpet sound his health.
**Heineken**  Is it a custom?
**Umlaut**  More honoured in the breach than the observance.

*Trumpets, cannon and orchestra playing "Deutschland über Alles" as before. All salute*

**Heineken**  The King is thirsty.
**Budweiser**  Look, see where it comes my lord!

*Enter Ghost accompanied by the customary jet of smoke and dragging his chain. He limps and holds his injured buttock*

**Umlaut**  My father to the life!

*Ghost beckons Umlaut to come apart from the others*

**Heineken**  It would speak with thee. Do not go.
**Umlaut**  I say away! Go on, I'll follow thee.

*Ghost beckons him away while the others retire*

Scene 4

**Ghost** Umlaut, I am thy father's ghost. Yes, I am thy vater-spook.
(*Fortunately pronounced "farter" in the German*)
**Umlaut** Vater!
**Ghost** Spook.
**Umlaut** Speak, spook.
**Ghost** Revenge my foul and most unnatural murder.
**Umlaut** Murder?
**Ghost** Murder most foul.
**Umlaut** Alas poor spook that you should suffer thus.
Tell me, that I with speedy wings may haste
To my revenge.
**Ghost** 'Tis given out that sleeping in my orchard
A serpent stung me.
But know thou noble youth
The serpent that did sting thy father's life
Now wears his crown.
**Umlaut** My uncle!
**Ghost** As I did sleep thy uncle stole to me.
And in the crevice of my ear did pour
A poisonous distilment, whose effect ——

*He breaks off as his visor suddenly falls down shut. He is blinded and gropes with difficulty round the stage, sometimes speaking with his back to Umlaut*

Oh horrible! Oh horrible! Most horrible!
If thou hast nature in thee bear it not.
Let not the royal bed of Düsseldorf
Be couch for luxury and damned incest.
But fare thee well
Adieu, adieu. Remember me.

*Blinded he cannot find the way out. Eventually Umlaut takes him by the arm and leads him off. Offstage we hear a voice cry "sod"*

**Umlaut** So Uncle, there you are. Now to my word.
I have sworn it.

*Enter Heineken and Budweiser*

**Budweiser**  My lord! My lord!
**Heineken**  Lord Umlaut!
**Budweiser**  What news my lord?
**Umlaut**  I'll tell thee more within, stout Budweiser.
   The time is out of joint. Oh cursed spite
   That ever I was born to set it right.

*Exeunt*

### Scene 5

*Enter Hildegard distressed. Enter Gezundheit meeting her*

**Gezundheit**  How now, Hildegard, what's the matter?
**Hildegard**  Oh my lord, I have been so affrighted!
**Gezundheit**  With what in the name of God?
**Hildegard**  My lord, as I was sewing in my closet
   The Lord Umlaut, with doublet all unloosed,
   His stockings fouled and round his ankles fall'n,
   Comes before me, with wild and piteous look.
**Gezundheit**  Mad for thy love?
**Hildegard**  I fear it.
**Gezundheit**  Come, go with me. I will go seek the King.

*Exeunt*

### Scene 6

*Umlaut solitary, brooding. Enter Gezundheit*

**Gezundheit**  My lord, I have news for you. The actors are come hither.

*Music*

Scene 7

*Enter Players*

**Umlaut**  You are welcome masters, welcome all. (*Aside to First Player*) Can you play the murder of Gonzalo?
**First Player**  Aye, my lord.
**Umlaut**  We'll have it tomorrow night. (*He takes him aside*) Could you insert a short scene which I would write for you?
**First Player**  Aye, my lord.
**Umlaut**  Excellent. Follow that lord and mock him not.

*Exeunt all except Umlaut*

If it were done when 'tis done then 'twere well
It were done quickly. The play's the thing
Wherein I'll catch the conscience of the king.

*Exit*


### Scene 7

*Enter King, Queen, Gezundheit and Hildegard*

**King**  We have sent for Umlaut to come hither
So he, as though by accident, may here
Affront Hildegard while we ourselves do watch.
We will bestow ourselves.
**Gezundheit**  I hear him coming. Let's withdraw, my lord.

*Exeunt all but Hildegard who stands to one side*

*Enter Umlaut. This is Umlaut's big moment and he is well aware he is about to say the most famous soliloquy in the English language. He dramatically takes up position and pauses*

**Umlaut**  To be or not to be, that is the question. (*Once again he pauses dramatically*)

Whether 'tis nobler ——

*He pauses because a jet of smoke is shooting across from* L

In the mind ——

*He stops because he is aware of Ghost marching on* R. *Ghost takes a few steps and then realizes he should have come on* L *with the smoke ("why didn't somebody tell me they had altered it"?). He retires hastily*

*Umlaut struggles on*

— to suffer
The slings and arrows of outrageous fortune
Or to take arms against a sea of troubles
And by opposing end them.

*Once more he pauses dramatically*

*This time Ghost appears* L *where the smoke came from*

*Unfortunately a jet of smoke then shoots forth from* R. *Ghost pauses in horror. Umlaut tries surreptitiously to shoo him away*

*Eventually Ghost takes the hint and withdraws* L

To die, to sleep;
No more; and by a sleep to say we end
The heart-ache and the thousand natural shocks
The flesh is heir to, 'tis a consummation
Devoutly to be wished. (*He pauses dramatically again*)

*Suddenly two jets of smoke appear, one* L, *one* R

*Ghost enters* C

Scene 7

**Ghost**  O, revenge me, Umlaut.

*Ghost exits*

*Umlaut is showing signs of strain but battles on*

**Umlaut**  To die, to sleep
 No more — perchance to dream; aye there's the rub
 For in that sleep of death what dreams may come ——

*The cannon, drums and "Deutschland über Alles" of the King's drinking salute sound, drowning out Umlaut. He shouts desperately through the din*

 — when we have shuffled off this mortal coil,
 Must give us pause. There's the respect
 That makes calamity of so long life.

*Once more he makes the fatal mistake of a long pause and totters round the stage indicating distress by biting the back of his hand*

*He pauses so long that Hildegard thinks he has dried and makes her entrance prematurely, carrying a large Valentine card*

**Hildegard**  My lord ——
**Umlaut**  (*with savage emphasis, glaring at her*)
 For who would bear the whips and
 Scorns of time

*Hildegard hastily exits*

 The oppressor's wrong, the proud man's contumely
 The pangs of despised love, the law's delay
 The insolence of office and the spurns
 That patient merit of the unworthy takes
 When he himself might his quietus make
 With a bare bodkin.

*Once more he pauses to roam the stage*

*A nervous Hildegard thinks he has finished, entering*

**Hildegard**  My Lord, I have remembrances of yours that I have ——

*Furious at being interrupted yet again in the greatest speech of his career, Umlaut loses control*

**Umlaut**  (*desperately*) Oh, get thee to a nunnery.

*He storms out and we hear him shout "I resign" in the wings*

*Hildegard is left stranded alone. After one or two sheepish grins and titters she cuts to the end*

**Hildegard**  Woe is me,
 To have seen what I have seen, see what I see.

*Hildegard slinks off*

## Scene 8

*Two thrones are set*

*Trumpets, drums etc.*

*Enter King, Queen, Gezundheit, Umlaut and Hildegard with Courtiers including Cup Bearer who now wears an eye patch or similar sign of injury*

**King**  Let the players come forth. Let the play commence. But first a toast. The King drinks to Umlaut.

*Cup Bearer produces a goblet. Trumpets, drums, cannon and "Deutschland über Alles". All salute and stand to attention. Screech.*

# Scene 8

*King throws his goblet away into the face of his long-suffering Cup Bearer*

*Enter Player*

*The hubbub dies away*

**A Player**  A prologue.

*Player bows and exits*

*Trumpets*

*Dumb show follows. This must be done swiftly so it does not drag. A flicker effect might be used to give the effect of a silent film*

*Enter Players wearing crowns as a king and queen, very loving and embracing.*

*The Player King carries on a strip of property grass, lays it down, yawns and lies down to sleep on it*

*The Player Queen kisses him and seeing him asleep leaves him*

*Another Player, the Poisoner, sneaks in, takes off the crown, kisses it and pours poison in the Player King's ear, using a large bottle and a funnel. He goes*

*The Player Queen returns and finds the Player King dead. She is distraught*

*The Poisoner returns and comforts her. The Player King crawls off, then crawls back for the grass*

*The Poisoner woos the Player Queen, giving her gifts. She rejects him at first but in the end lets him kiss her and accepts his love*

*Exeunt dumb show*

*There is a general murmur among the spectators. Suddenly the King rises*

**King**  Give o'er the play!

*At this point Ghost arrives accompanied by his usual cloud of smoke. Nobody can see Ghost except Umlaut and the King*

**Ghost**  Umlaut. Revenge me.
**King**  Which of you has done this? Thou canst not say I did it. Never shake thy gory locks at me.
**Ghost**  Revenge me, Umlaut. Oh revenge!

*Once more his visor comes down with a snap. He gropes in the fog looking for a way out.*

**King**  Give me some light! Away!
**Gezundheit**  Lights, lights!

*Attendants bring on torches or lanterns*

*The King storms out followed by everybody else except Umlaut and Heineken*

*Ghost vainly gropes for an exit and nearly falls off the stage*

**Umlaut**  What frighted with false fire? Did'st perceive?
**Heineken**  Very well, my lord.
**Umlaut**  Upon the poisoning?
**Heineken**  I did very well note him.
**Umlaut**  I'll take the ghost's word for a thousand pounds ... (*His voice dies away as he realizes Ghost is still blundering about the stage*)

*A female ASM stretches out an arm and drags Ghost off savagely*

Scene 9

**Ghost**  Whurp!

*Enter Gezundheit*

**Umlaut**  God bless you, sir.
**Gezundheit**  My lord, the Queen would speak with you in her closet.
**Umlaut**  I will come by and by.
**Gezundheit**  I will say so.

*Gezundheit exits*

**Umlaut**  Now for my mother.

*Umlaut exits*

### Scene 9

*Enter King with Rosenstern and Guildencranz*

**King**  I like him not, nor stands it safe with us
   To let his madness range.
   Therefore prepare you worthy Rosenstern and Guildencranz
   Umlaut must thus be safely made with speed.
   You take my drift?
**Rosenstern**
**Guildencranz**  } (*together*) My lord?
**King**  Death. A grave.
**Rosenstern**
**Guildencranz**  } (*together*) He shall not live.
**King**  I your commission will forthwith dispatch.
   He shall to Norway with you both
   But not return. You understand?
**Rosenstern**
**Guildencranz**  } (*together*) Ja wohl my lord.
**King**  Then farewell trusty Rosenstern and gallant Guildencranz.

*Rosenstern and Guildencranz salute and exit*

*Enter Gezundheit*

**Gezundheit**  My lord he's going to his mother's closet.
Behind the arras I'll convey myself
To hear the process. Farewell my liege.
I'll call upon you 'ere you go to bed
And tell you what I know.

*Exit Gezundheit*

**King**  Oh my offence is rank. It smells to heaven.
And yet I cannot pray.
Wherefore cannot I say amen?
I'll try to pray once more. (*He kneels*)

*Enter Umlaut who, seeing the King, comes threateningly behind him*

**Umlaut**  Now might I do it pat. (*He goes to pull out dagger, but it sticks in its sheath. He tugs furiously and the handle comes away in his hand*)
Is this a — er — handle that I see before me?
I see the gouts of blood upon thy blade — er — handle.
I must ... er ... I shall ... I think I'll go and see my mother.

*Umlaut exits*

**King**  My words fly up, my thoughts remain below.
Words without thoughts never to heaven go.

*King exits*

## Scene 10

*The Queen's closet*

*There is an arras on both sides of the stage*

*Enter Queen and Gezundheit*

**Gezundheit**  Pray be round with him.
**Queen**  Fear not. Withdraw. I hear him coming.

*Gezundheit hides behind the arras*

  *Enter Umlaut*

**Queen**  Umlaut, thou hast thy father much offended.
**Umlaut**  What's the matter now?
**Queen**  Have you forgot me?
**Umlaut**  You are the Queen, your husband's brother's wife
  And would it were not so you are my mother. (*He seizes her*)
**Queen**  What wilt thou do? Thou wilt not murder me? Help ho!
**Gezundheit**  (*from behind the arras*) What ho. Help!
**Umlaut**  How now? A rat? Dead for a ducat, dead! (*He draws his dagger and then realizes it has no blade. He is dumbstruck for a moment and then runs to the arras and kicks it savagely*) Die dog!

*Unfortunately he has attacked the arras in the wrong place. Gezundheit falls dead out of the arras on the other side of the stage*

**Gezundheit**  Oh I am slain!
**Queen**  What hast thou done?
**Umlaut**  Nay I know not. Is it the King? (*He recognizes Gezundheit*)
  Thou wretched rash intruding fool, farewell.
  I took thee for thy better.

  *Ghost enters with the usual dense fog*

**Umlaut**  What would you have me do?
**Ghost**  Umlaut! This visitation is to whet thy blunted purpose. Revenge me!
**Umlaut**  My thoughts are nothing else but for revenge.
**Queen**  To whom do you speak?
**Umlaut**  Do you see nothing there? It is the vater-spook.
**Queen**  Nothing at all. (*She coughs in the smoke*)
**Umlaut**  Look you there. See how it steals away!
My father in his armour as he lived!

*Ghost is having his usual trouble with the visor. He trips over Gezundheit as he goes. He crawls off*

Mother, good-night. I'll put Gezundheit in the room next door. Good-night, Mother.

*Exit, dragging Gezundheit. He picks him up by the shoulders to drag him but that doesn't work so he takes his feet and savagely pulls him out, to complaints from Gezundheit*

**Queen**  Alas, he's mad. What shall I do?

*Black-out*

### Scene 11

*Enter King, Rosenstern and Guildencranz, Umlaut and Attendants including Cup Bearer wearing a bloodstained bandage or plaster on his face*

**King**  Umlaut this deed must send thee hence with fiery quickness.
**Umlaut**  For Norway?
**King**  Aye, Umlaut.
**Umlaut**  Good.
**King**  It will be good for all of us.
**Umlaut**  For Norway! Farewell.

Scene 12

*Umlaut exits*

**King** (*to Rosenstern and Guildencranz*)
Follow him. I'll have him hence tonight.
You have my letter to the Norway king
Which will import the present death of Hamlet.
Do it Norway.
**Rosenstern**
**Guildencranz** } (*together*) Ja wohl!

*They salute and exit*

**King**   Give me a cup. I'll drink to that. (*He snatches a goblet from his Cup Bearer and drinks. As usual he throws the empty cup at the Cup Bearer*)

*Cannons roar, drums, "Deutschland über Alles"*

*During this King exits while all salute and stand to attention*

### Scene 12

*There is a small stage bush flat on stage made of canvas with rosemary and flowers pinned to it*

*Enter Hildegard, mad. Her dress is disordered. She is draped with a string of runner beans with a few weeds in it. She gaily starts to pick flowers*

**Hildegard**   There's pansies, that's for thoughts ... there's rosemary, that's for remembrance.

*The pansy comes off freely but unfortunately the rosemary has been nailed to the flat by an over-enthusiastic ASM ("nobody told me she had to pick the bloody thing"). She tugs without result. She tugs harder. The flat falls over. She stands indecisive and then inspiration strikes*

Oh look! There is a willow grows aslant the brook. I'll take a look.

*She runs off*

*There is a short pause and then the sound of a large splash offstage, followed by a bubbling noise as of a large object sinking*

*Black-out*

SCENE 13

*An empty stage*

*A thunderous knocking*

*Enter drunken Porter, holding a huge key*

**Porter** Here's a knocking indeed. If a man were porter of Hell Gate he should have old turning the key.

*Exit Porter*

*Enter King and Queen*

**King** Whence comes that knocking?

*Sound of loud hubbub*

*Grolsch bursts in but the knocking continues*

**Grolsch** Where is the King?

*The knocking stops abruptly*

Vile king, give me my father. (*He seizes him by the throat*)
**Queen** Calmly good Grolsch.
**Grolsch** Where is my father?

Scene 15

**King** Dead.
**Grolsch** And where is my sister Hildegard?
**Queen** Mad.
**Grolsch** How came they so?
**King** Your father murderéd by Umlaut was,
   Your sister mad with grief and unrequited love
   For that same person.
**Grolsch** Oh horror! But my revenge will come.
**King** Where the offence is let the great axe fall. I pray you go with me.

*Exeunt*


SCENE 14

*Enter Heineken, reading a letter*

**Heineken** From Umlaut! "Heineken I am returned. There was a storm and the ship sank. Rosenstern and Guildencranz were thrown overboard to lighten the ship and I alone escaped by a miracle. Let the King know and I will greet thee tomorrow".

*Exit*


SCENE 15

*Enter King and Grolsch*

**King** We loved your father as we love ourself
   And he which hath your noble father slain
   Pursued my life.
**Grolsch** So it appears. But what's to do?
**King** We shall arrange a friendly bout of foils.
   An accident may well occur to Umlaut. (*He winks and nudges Grolsch*)
**Grolsch** I have the very thing.

I'll use a poison that I bought in France.
And with that I will annoint my sword.
**King** Away, and mock the time with fairest show.
False face must hide what a false heart doth know.

*Enter Queen weeping*

**Queen** Oh treble woe. Hildegard's dead.
**Grolsch** My sister dead? How?
**Queen** Drowned, drowned. While mad she fell into the brook and sank.
**Grolsch** (*weeping*) She should have died hereafter.
There would have been a time for such a word.
**King** All this is Umlaut's work. Come let's away
To think upon the horrors of this day.

*Exeunt*

## Scene 16

*A graveyard*

*A Clown is discovered digging. If there is no trap in the stage the grave can be built up using canvas on a frame. He throws up a huge bone about two feet long. Props couldn't find a skull*

*Umlaut and Heineken enter*

**Umlaut** Who did that bone belong to?
**Clown** To Boracic, the old king's wrestling champion.
**Umlaut** What part of him was it?
**Clown** His thumb.
**Umlaut** His thumb?
**Clown** He had large hands.
**Umlaut** Alas, poor Boracic. Thou art now only a bone.

## Scene 16

*Enter King, Queen, Grolsch and Hildegard on a stretcher carried by two Bier-Carriers plus Lords and Ladies. Queen carries flowers*

*Umlaut and Heineken withdraw*

**Grolsch**  Lay her in the earth
And from her fair and unpolluted flesh
May violets spring.
**Umlaut**  What, the fair Hildegard?

*The two Bier-Carriers take up position at each end of the grave and lower the stretcher, but it is too long to go into the grave. An embarrassed pause. Everybody tries to cover up by crossing themselves frequently. Law 17 of Coarse Acting: when in trouble in Shakespeare cross yourself. The Bier-Carriers make signals to each other and hit upon a solution. Each takes a downstage corner of the stretcher and lifts it up, thus rolling Hildegard into the grave. Queen scatters flowers over the grave*

**Queen**  Sweets to the sweet! Farewell.
**Grolsch**  Hold off the earth a while 'til I have caught her once more in mine arms. (*He leaps into the grave*).
**Umlaut**  What is he whose grief
Bears such an emphasis. I loved Hildegard. (*He also leaps into the grave*)

*From the tomb comes a shriek as Umlaut lands on Hildegard. She struggles out of the grave. She dusts herself down and then assumes the posture of a vertical corpse with closed eyes and arms crossed piously on her chest. Taking little steps to show she's not really alive, she shuffles back to the grave. Umlaut and Grolsch are still standing there swaying with hands round each other's throats. She motions them to get out and they do so. She carefully climbs into the grave, sits upright in it, still keeping up her corpse routine and then sinks from sight*

**King**  Oh he is mad, Grolsch.
**Queen**  For love of God forebear ——

*She is briefly interrupted by Hildegard throwing out of the grave a saw she had obviously been lying on*

— to kill him, Umlaut.
**King**  I pray thee, noble Heineken, take him hence.

*Exeunt Umlaut and Heineken*

Come now good Grolsch attend me to my chamber.
We will discuss those things we talked of earlier.
I pray you come.

*Exeunt all except Hildegard*

*The Lights should fade but a spot on the grave remains. Embarrassed silence*

*Then Hildegard climbs out after a preliminary peek and goes off in her corpse-like walk*

## Scene 17

*Enter Umlaut and Heineken*

**Heineken**  So Rosenstern and Guildencranz are dead.
**Umlaut**  Why man, they did make love to this employment. They are not near my conscience.

*Enter Anthrax. He wears an ornate hat with several feathers in it. He sweeps this off as he bows and all the feathers come out*

**Anthrax**  My lord, my name is Anthrax. His Majesty bid me signify he has laid a great wager on your head if you would contest some passes at swords with Grolsch.
**Umlaut**  Well, honest Anthrax, I will walk here in the hall and await Grolsch and the king.
**Anthrax**  I commend my duty to his lordship.

## Scene 17

*Anthrax exits, picking up a feather or two*

**Heineken**  You will lose this wager.
**Umlaut**  I do not think so.
**Heineken**  I can send to say you are not fit.
**Umlaut**  Not a whit.
If it were done when 'tis done then 'twere well
'Twere done quickly.

*Trumpets and drums etc.*

*Enter Attendants with chairs, a table plus drinks, a bucket and weapons etc. including fencing swords, and Cup Bearer who is showing signs of further injury*

*Enter King and Queen with Grolsch*

**King**  Come Umlaut, take this hand from me. (*He puts Grolsch's hand into Umlaut's*)
**Umlaut**  I embrace it freely. Give us the foils, come on.

*They take their swords. Grolsch chooses one but the King shakes his head*

**Grolsch**  This is too heavy. Let me see another.

*The King secretly indicates one which he takes*

**King**  If Umlaut give the first or second hit
The King shall drink to Umlaut's better health.
Now the King drinks to Umlaut.

*The usual cannon, drums and music. The King throws his goblet at the Cup Bearer as usual. All salute and stand to attention*

Come, begin. And you the judges bear a wary eye.
**Umlaut**  Come on, sir.

**Grolsch**  Come, my lord.

*Grolsch advances and as he does he puts his foot into the small bucket by the table. He tries to shake it off without success but has to start the fight with it on his leg. The fight is desperately quick and mechanical, probably the only bit they rehearsed properly. Just three or four parries and thrusts carried out at great speed*

**Umlaut**  One.
**Grolsch**  No.
**Umlaut**  Judgement?
**Anthrax**  A hit. A very palpable hit.

*Grolsch at last gets rid of the bucket*

**Grolsch**  Come again.
**King**  Umlaut, this pearl is thine
  Here's to thy health. Give him the cup.

*He drops a pearl into the cup*

**Umlaut**  I'll play this bout first. Set it by.

*They fight. The fight is exactly the same as the first fight, with the same moves and business*

  Another hit what say you?
**Grolsch**  A touch. I do confess.
**Queen**  The Queen carouses to thy fortune, Umlaut.

*Queen takes the cup with a pearl in it*

**King**  Wilhelmina, do not drink.
**Queen**  I will my lord. I pray you pardon me. (*She drinks*)
**King**  (*aside*) It is the poisoned cup. Too late!
**Grolsch**  (*aside to king*) My lord, I'll hit him now.
**Umlaut**  Come for the third, Grolsch. You do but dally.
**Grolsch**  Say you so? Come on.

Scene 17

*They play exactly as before*

**Anthrax**  Nothing either way.
**Grolsch**  Look behind thee, my lord.

*Umlaut lowers his sword and turns round. Grolsch gives him a quick stab in the back*

   Have at you now.
**Umlaut**  (*dropping out of character*) Ouch! That hurt!

*He furiously attacks Grolsch using his sword like a whip. Grolsch throws away his sword and flees, ending up cowering on the floor shielding his face with his hands. After a brief initial struggle Umlaut manages to control himself and gets back into character. He throws Grolsch his own sword and picks up Grolsch's. They resume a fencing position with Grolsch extremely scared and keeping as far away as he can, and flinching at every parry*

   Nay, come again.

*The Queen gives a cry and falls*

**Anthrax**  Look to the Queen there!

*Attendants help the Queen. They fight as before. This time after one parry Grolsch lifts his upstage arm high in the air. Umlaut places his sword under Grolsch's armpit and Grolsch drops his arm to his side ("The Royal Shakespeare Armpit Death"). Umlaut thrusts with his sword and then withdraws it. Grolsch gives a ghastly cry and staggers round the stage groaning and fiddling with his blood capsule which is unfortunately down by his downstage groin ("I thought he was going to stick it in you down there"). Eventually he gets it to work and sinks to the floor spouting blood*

   How is it, Grolsch?
**Grolsch**  (*holding his groin*) I am justly killed by my own treachery.
**Umlaut**  How fares the Queen?

**King**  She swoons to see them bleed.
**Queen**  No, no. The drink, the drink. Oh my dear Umlaut,
The drink, the drink. I am poisoned. (*She dies at some length, rising from her chair and using the whole stage. "Well it was my big chance"*)
**Grolsch**  Umlaut, thou too art slain.
In thee there is not half an hour of life.
The treacherous instrument is in thy hand.
Envenomed with a poison on the blade.
Thy mother's poisoned too.
The King's to blame.
**Umlaut**  The point envenomed? Then venom to thy work. (*He stabs the King*)
**King**  Oh yet defend me friends. I am but hurt.
**Umlaut**  Here thou incestuous murderer.
Drink of this potion. (*He forces the King to drink*)

*Bang on cue the invisible royal orchestra and the cannon and drums sound their usual signal. All stand to attention and salute except the dead and dying. Cup Bearer kneels beside the King*

Follow my mother.

*The King dies but with a last effort manages to throw his goblet at the battered face of his Cup Bearer who is kneeling beside him. Cup Bearer drops dead*

**Grolsch**  He is justly served.
It is a poison tempered by himself.
Exchange forgiveness with me, noble Umlaut. (*He dies*)

*Umlaut totters and falls*

**Umlaut**  Noble Heineken, I am dead and thou live'st.
Report me and my cause aright
To the unsatisfied.
I die, Heineken.

Scene 17

*Umlaut makes one of his famous silences and Heineken, thinking he has dried, jumps in*

**Heineken**  Let two captains ——
**Umlaut**  (*sitting up*) The rest is silence. (*He dies at last*)
**Heineken**  Let two captains
   Bear Umlaut like a soldier to the stage
   And for his passage let the soldiers' drums
   Speak loudly for him.

*All stand with bowed heads*

*Two Attendants place Umlaut on a stretcher and solemnly march off stage to a drum beat. They have difficulty avoiding the scattered corpses and the Queen's body has to move itself out of the way*

*A puff of smoke and Ghost appears in a spot. Silence. Ghost has forgotten the last line in the play. He sidles nearer the wings*

**Ghost**  (*out of the corner of his mouth*) Yes?
**Prompt**  Revenge.
**Ghost**  Ah yes, revenge!

*Grim music, probably Wagner*

*The Lights fade*

CURTAIN

# FURNITURE AND PROPERTY LIST

## Scene 1

*On stage*: Lance (for **Budweiser**)

*Off stage*: Lance (**Heineken**)
Lance (**Kronenbourg**)
Long length of chain (**Ghost**)

## Scene 2

*Set*: Two thrones

*Off stage*: Huge goblet of wine made of papier mâché or similar (**Cup Bearer**)

## Scene 3

*Strike*: Thrones

## Scene 4

*Off stage*: Long length of chain (**Ghost**)

## Scene 5

As before

## Scene 6

As before

Furniture and Property List

### Scene 7

*Off stage*: Long length of chain (**Ghost**)
Valentine card (**Hildegard**)

### Scene 8

*Set*: Two thrones

*Off stage*: Goblet (**Cup Bearer**)
Strip of property grass (**Player King**)
Large bottle, funnel, gifts (**Poisoner**)
Torches or lanterns (**Attendants**)

### Scene 9

*Strike*: Thrones

*Personal*: **Umlaut**: dagger with loose handle in sheath

### Scene 10

*Set*: Two arrases

### Scene 11

*Strike*: Arrases

*Off stage*: Goblet (**Cup Bearer**)

### Scene 12

*Set*: Small stage bush flat made of canvas with flowers and rosemary attached to it

### Scene 13

*Strike*: Small stage bush flat

| | |
|---|---|
| *Off stage*: | Huge key (**Porter**) |

## Scene 14

| | |
|---|---|
| *Off stage*: | Letter (**Heineken**) |

## Scene 15

As before

## Scene 16

| | |
|---|---|
| *Set*: | Grave. *In it*: saw, huge bone about two feet long |
| *Off stage*: | Stretcher (**Bier-Carriers**)<br>Flowers (**Queen**) |

## Scene 17

| | |
|---|---|
| *Strike*: | Grave, saw, bone |
| *Off stage*: | Chairs, table with drinks, a bucket and weapons etc. including fencing swords (**Attendants**)<br>Goblet (**Cup Bearer**)<br>Pearl (**King**)<br>Stretcher (**Attendants**) |
| *Personal*: | Blood capsule (**Grolsch**) |

# LIGHTING PLOT

Property fittings required: nil

*To open*: Darkness

| | | |
|---|---|---|
| *Cue* 1 | When ready<br>*Bring up Lights slowly* | (Page 1) |
| *Cue* 2 | **Ghost** enters<br>*Green spot on* **Ghost** | (Page 1) |
| *Cue* 3 | To accompany dumb show (optional)<br>*Strobe or flicker effect* | (Page 13) |
| *Cue* 4 | **Queen**: "What shall I do?"<br>*Black-out* | (Page 18) |
| *Cue* 5 | To open Scene 11<br>*Bring up Lights* | (Page 18) |
| *Cue* 6 | Exeunt all except **Hildegard**<br>*Fade Lights. Spot on grave* | (Page 24) |
| *Cue* 7 | To open Scene 17<br>*Bring up Lights* | (Page 24) |
| *Cue* 8 | **Ghost** enters<br>*Spot on* **Ghost** | (Page 29) |
| *Cue* 9 | Grim music plays<br>*Fade Lights* | (Page 29) |

# EFFECTS PLOT

| | | |
|---|---|---|
| *Cue* 1 | As the Lights come up<br>*Sound of howling wind. The stage is filled with smoke* | (Page 1) |
| *Cue* 2 | **Ghost** enters<br>*Puff of smoke to accompany* **Ghost** | (Page 1) |
| *Cue* 3 | **Heineken**: "Hic, haec, hoc."<br>*Cock crows* | (Page 2) |
| *Cue* 4 | To open S<small>CENE</small> 2<br>*A flourish sounds* | (Page 3) |
| *Cue* 5 | **Gezundheit** and **Grolsch** go to leave the stage<br>*Jet of smoke meets* **Gezundheit** *and* **Grolsch** | (Page 3) |
| *Cue* 6 | **King**: "Come away."<br>*Cannon and drums sound, followed by two bars of<br>"Deutschland über Alles", played at high speed.<br>Music ends in a screech* | (Page 4) |
| *Cue* 7 | **Umlaut**, **Heineken** and **Budweiser** enter<br>*Wind howls* | (Page 5) |
| *Cue* 8 | **Budweiser**: "No, it is struck."<br>*Sudden sound of trumpets, cannons and two or<br>three bars of "Deutschland über Alles", plus cheering* | (Page 6) |
| *Cue* 9 | **Umlaut**: "... than the observance."<br>*Sound of trumpets, cannons and "Deutschland über<br>Alles" as before* | (Page 6) |
| *Cue* 10 | **Ghost** enters<br>*Puff of smoke to accompany* **Ghost** | (Page 6) |

Effects Plot

| | | |
|---|---|---|
| *Cue* 11 | **Gezundheit**: "The actors are come hither."<br>*Music plays* | (Page 8) |
| *Cue* 12 | **Umlaut**: "Whether 'tis nobler —— "<br>*Jet of smoke from* L | (Page 10) |
| *Cue* 13 | **Ghost** enters from L<br>*Jet of smoke from* R | (Page 10) |
| *Cue* 14 | **Umlaut**: "Devoutly to be wished." Pause<br>*Two jets of smoke from both* R *and* L | (Page 10) |
| *Cue* 15 | **Umlaut**: "… what dreams may come —— "<br>*Cannon, drums and "Deutschland über Alles" sound* | (Page 11) |
| *Cue* 16 | To open SCENE 8<br>*Trumpets, drums etc. sound* | (Page 12) |
| *Cue* 17 | **Cup Bearer** produces a goblet<br>*Trumpets, drums and "Deutschland über Alles"*<br>*sound, followed by a screech* | (Page 13) |
| *Cue* 18 | **Player** bows and exits<br>*Trumpets sound* | (Page 13) |
| *Cue* 19 | **Ghost** enters<br>*Cloud of smoke to accompany* **Ghost** | (Page 14) |
| *Cue* 20 | **Ghost** enters<br>*Dense fog of smoke to accompany* **Ghost** | (Page 17) |
| *Cue* 21 | **King** throws goblet at **Cup Bearer**<br>*Cannons roar, drums and "Deutschland über Alles"* | (Page 19) |
| *Cue* 22 | **Hildegard** runs off. Pause<br>*Large splash followed by a bubbling noise* | (Page 20) |
| *Cue* 23 | To open SCENE 13<br>*Thunderous knocking which continues* | (Page 20) |

| | | |
|---|---|---|
| *Cue* 24 | **King**: "Whence comes that knocking?"<br>*Sound of loud hubub* | (Page 20) |
| *Cue* 25 | **Grolsch**: "Where is the King?"<br>*Knocking stops abruptly* | (Page 20) |
| *Cue* 26 | **Umlaut**: "'Twere done quickly."<br>*Trumpets and drums etc.* | (Page 25) |
| *Cue* 27 | **King**: "Now the King drinks to Umlaut."<br>*Usual cannons, drums and music* | (Page 25) |
| *Cue* 28 | **Umlaut** forces the **King** to drink<br>*Usual cannons, drums and music* | (Page 28) |
| *Cue* 29 | **Attendants** march off with **Umlaut** on the stretcher<br>*Drum beat* | (Page 29) |
| *Cue* 30 | **Ghost** enters<br>*Puff of smoke to accompany* **Ghost** | (Page 29) |
| *Cue* 31 | **Ghost**: "Ah yes, revenge!"<br>*Grim music, probably Wagner* | (Page 29) |

www.ingramcontent.com/pod-product-compliance
Lightning Source LLC
Chambersburg PA
CBHW070453050426
42450CB00012B/3252